ALISHA KAPANI

Quantum Physics for Kids

Explore Atoms, Molecules, & the Magic of Matter with Fun Activities & Experiments for Curious Young Minds, Ages 5+

Copyright © 2024 by Alisha Kapani

All rights reserved. No part of this publication may be reproduced, stored or transmitted in any form or by any means, electronic, mechanical, photocopying, recording, scanning, or otherwise without written permission from the publisher. It is illegal to copy this book, post it to a website, or distribute it by any other means without permission.

Alisha Kapani asserts the moral right to be identified as the author of this work.

Alisha Kapani has no responsibility for the persistence or accuracy of URLs for external or third-party Internet Websites referred to in this publication and does not guarantee that any content on such Websites is, or will remain, accurate or appropriate.

Designations used by companies to distinguish their products are often claimed as trademarks. All brand names and product names used in this book and on its cover are trade names, service marks, trademarks and registered trademarks of their respective owners. The publishers and the book are not associated with any product or vendor mentioned in this book. None of the companies referenced within the book have endorsed the book.

First edition

This book was professionally typeset on Reedsy.
Find out more at reedsy.com

Contents

Introduction: Welcome to the Quantum World!	1
Chapter 1: What's an Atom?	3
Chapter 2: Inside the Atom Adventure!	6
Chapter 3: The Magic of Molecules!	9
Chapter 4: The Wonderful World of Matter!	11
Chapter 5: Schrödinger's Curious Cat: An Unusual Tale	13
Chapter 6: Exploring Uncertainty and Duality: A Playful...	17
Chapter 7: Unraveling the Double-Slit Mystery: A Fun...	21
Chapter 8: Quantum Superposition: The Wondrous Trick of...	25
Chapter 9: Quantum Entanglement: The Incredible Twin...	29
Conclusion: Our Quantum Journey!	33
Bonus Experiments: Uncover the Magic of Quantum Physics!	36
References	39

Introduction: Welcome to the Quantum World!

Welcome, curious minds, to a realm of tiny wonders and fantastic discoveries—the amazing world of quantum physics! Have you ever wondered what makes everything around us so magical and exciting? Well, get ready to dive into a universe where the tiniest particles and incredible forces come together to create the world we see!

Imagine a world where things can be in two places at once, where particles talk to each other from far away, and where even a cat can be both asleep and awake at the same time! It might sound a bit puzzling at first, but don't worry—our journey through the quantum world is going to be filled with fun and wonder.

In this book, we'll embark on a fantastic adventure to explore atoms, the building blocks of everything, and how they team up to create magical things called molecules. We'll uncover the secrets of matter and how it can change shapes, from solid ice to melty chocolate, and discover the incredible stories behind some mind-boggling experiments!

But that's not all! We're going to delve into some really cool ideas that might make you scratch your head a bit. We'll talk about a clever cat, some tricky games of hide and seek with particles, and even perform experiments in our minds where things happen in ways we'd never expect!

So, are you ready to join us on this incredible adventure into the mysterious and magical world of quantum physics? Get your imagination ready, because we're about to discover some of the most amazing things our universe has to offer!

Get set, quantum adventurers! Our journey is about to begin!

Chapter 1: What's an Atom?

Imagine a tiny building block that makes everything!

Welcome, curious minds! Today, we're going to embark on an incredible journey into the heart of the smallest things in our universe—atoms! Imagine that everything you see, touch, or even imagine is made up of these tiny, super-duper small building blocks called atoms.

Let's take a moment to think about a world where everything is made up of these little building blocks. Picture your favorite toys, your pets, even the air we breathe—all made of countless numbers of these tiny, invisible particles!

Atoms as Building Blocks

So, what exactly are atoms? Well, atoms are like the building blocks of a giant LEGO castle or the tiny beads in your favorite bracelet. They're so small that you can't see them with your eyes, but they're incredibly important because they make up everything around us!

Imagine atoms as super tiny balls. These balls are so small that if you lined up a billion of them, they'd only be about as wide as the dot on this page! They're the basic units that make up everything in the whole wide world.

Atoms are like LEGO blocks or marbles!

Think of atoms as those magical LEGO blocks you love to build with. Each atom is like a single LEGO block, and when you put many atoms together, just like when you connect many LEGO blocks, they create something new and amazing!

Or, imagine atoms as tiny marbles. When you collect lots of marbles and put them together in different ways, they can create all sorts of things—just like how atoms come together to create everything around us!

Activity: Let's Build an Atom!

Are you ready for some fun? Let's create our own atom using colorful playdough or by drawing one! Imagine an atom has a round center called the nucleus. Let's make a small ball for the nucleus. Around the nucleus, add some tiny balls or sticks to represent the electrons moving around it. Voila! You've created your very own atom!

Chapter 1: What's an Atom?

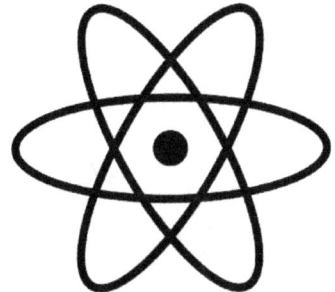

Chapter 2: Inside the Atom Adventure!

Let's shrink and explore inside an atom!

Welcome back, explorers! Last time, we discovered that everything around us is made up of tiny building blocks called atoms. Now, it's time to journey inside these amazing atoms and find out what's hiding within!

Introduction to Protons, Neutrons, and Electrons

Imagine atoms as tiny solar systems! At the center of our atom-world are these special, super-tiny parts called protons and neutrons. These are like the stars and planets, and they're snuggled together in a place we call the nucleus.

And zooming around the nucleus, like speedy comets, are even tinier particles called electrons. They zip around the nucleus in special paths called orbits.

Chapter 2: Inside the Atom Adventure!

Playful Visualization

Think of the nucleus as a cozy group of friends huddling together in the middle of a big playground. The protons and neutrons stick close together, like the best pals they are, while the electrons whizz around them, playing a never-ending game of tag!

Activity: Balloon and Confetti Party!

Are you ready for a bit of fun with electricity? Grab a balloon and rub it on your hair or a cozy sweater. Now, hold the balloon close to some tiny bits of paper or confetti. Watch what happens! The confetti will stick to the balloon, just like electrons stick to atoms because of something called electric charge!

Wow, wasn't it amazing to see how the balloon could attract the confetti? That's a bit like how electrons and atoms play together! Next time, we'll dive into how these playful atoms team up to create fantastic things called molecules!

Chapter 3: The Magic of Molecules!

Imagine atoms holding hands and making something new!

Welcome back, curious minds! Last time, we ventured inside atoms and met their tiny inhabitants—protons, neutrons, and electrons. Today, get ready to witness the fantastic team-up of these atoms as they create something truly magical—molecules!

Picture molecules as teams of atoms working together, just like a squad of friends joining hands to create something amazing! When atoms hold hands—or more accurately, share their electrons—they form these wonderful groups called molecules.

Examples of Familiar Molecules

Think about the air you breathe or the water you drink—these are all made up of molecules! For instance, water (H_2O) is a fantastic team of two hydrogen atoms and one oxygen atom. Even the air we breathe, which is mostly made of oxygen molecules (O_2), is created by teams of oxygen atoms working together.

Activity: Mix and See!

Let's have some colorful fun! Take two glasses of water—one with red food coloring and the other with blue. Carefully pour them into a third glass. What do you see? The colors mix and swirl together, just like how atoms come together to create new colors in molecules!

Wow, isn't it amazing how atoms join forces to create these marvelous molecules? Next time, we'll explore how these incredible molecules play a big role in creating different forms of matter—solid, liquid, and gas!

Chapter 4: The Wonderful World of Matter!

Imagine matter as a shape-shifter!

Welcome back, explorers! We've uncovered the secret teams of atoms forming fantastic molecules. Now, let's delve deeper into the enchanting world of matter—where things can change shape, size, and even how they feel!

Definition of Matter: Anything That Takes Up Space and Has Mass

Think of matter as the stuff that fills up space and feels different to touch. Whether it's your favorite toy, a soft pillow, or the air you breeze through, it's all matter! Anything that takes up space and has weight is made of matter.

Solid, Liquid, and Gas States

Matter can transform into three main forms: solids, liquids, and gases. Imagine a solid as something you can hold, like a rock or your toys. A liquid, like water, can flow and take the shape of its container. And gas, like the air we breathe, can fill any space it's given!

Activity: Matter Changing Its Form!

Let's have some hands-on fun with matter! Take an ice cube and watch it melt in your hand or put it under the sun. What happens? The ice changes from solid to liquid! You can also melt chocolate and then let it cool back into a solid. That's matter changing its form!

See how matter can change from solid to liquid to gas? Isn't that fascinating? In the next chapter, we'll dive into some super exciting ideas about cats, uncertainty, and some really curious experiments that might leave you scratching your head!

Chapter 5: Schrödinger's Curious Cat: An Unusual Tale

Once upon a time, in a house filled with cozy nooks and sunlit spots, there lived a special cat named Schrödinger. Now, Schrödinger wasn't your ordinary feline—he was an extraordinary cat of paradoxes, where naps and adventures danced together in a most peculiar way.

Paws and Possibilities

Picture a fluffy cat nestled in a sunny corner, peacefully snoozing away with his eyes closed tight. But wait, something curious happens! While Schrödinger dreamt of chasing cosmic mice or taking grand leaps among twinkling stars, he was also exploring the house, chasing yarn and playing hide-and-seek with invisible friends. How can he be asleep and awake all at once? It's a puzzle of playful possibilities!

Dreamy Adventures Unravel

As the sunbeams painted patterns on the floor, Schrödinger's dreams and his wide-eyed escapades began to blur. In his dreams, he'd soar through quantum realms, hopping between alternate universes, chasing rainbows made of stardust. Meanwhile, in reality, he'd scamper around, paws batting at imaginary wonders—two adventures intertwined into one!

Purr-fect Paradox Unleashed

Now, imagine Schrödinger's human friends—they couldn't quite understand their furry companion's peculiar behavior. "Is he asleep?" they'd wonder. "Or is he wide awake?" It was a delightful puzzle for everyone in the house, a whimsical mystery wrapped in a purring, fuzzy bundle of fun!

Tails of Sleepy-Wakefulness

In Schrödinger's world, a doze and a frolic could twirl together, making his adventures a magical blend of dreams and reality. He'd nap, whiskers twitching to imaginary tales, while simultaneously galloping across the house in playful pursuit of invisible wonders. It was as if his dreams tiptoed into his wakeful moments, creating a joyous, puzzling dance of sleepiness and alertness!

Schrödinger's Whisker-twirling Tale

In the enchanting tale of Schrödinger's curious cat life, dreams and wakefulness swirled together like colors on an artist's palette. His playful paradox became a charming mystery, leaving everyone with giggles and grins, marveling at the delightful confusion of a cat both asleep and wide awake. And as the sun set, Schrödinger curled up, whiskers twitching to tales unknown, ready to embark on another whimsical journey of paradoxical adventures in dreamland and reality!

Activity: Cat's Nap Hide-and-Seek

Materials Needed:

- Stuffed toy cat or a picture of a cat
- A small box or a toy bed for the cat
- A soft blanket or a cloth to cover the cat

Activity Steps:

- 1. **Meet Schrödinger's Cat:** Introduce the child to the stuffed toy cat or show them a picture of a cute cat. Explain that this cat is special and sometimes does something very surprising!
- 2. **Cat's Sleeping Spot:** Show the child the small box or toy bed and place the cat inside it. Explain that the cat loves to take naps and sometimes likes to hide in its cozy spot.
- 3. **Cat's Mystery Nap:** Cover the box or bed with the soft blanket or cloth, making it a cozy hiding place for the cat. Explain that while the cat is hidden, it's taking a nap, but it might also be awake at the same time!
- 4. **Guess the Cat's State:** Ask the child to guess whether the cat is napping or playing while it's hidden. Encourage them to imagine what the cat might be doing inside without peeking.
- 5. **Reveal the Surprise:** After a short while, remove the cloth and show the cat in its hiding spot. Discuss with the child how they guessed the cat's state while it was hidden. Emphasize that until they saw the cat, it was both napping and awake in a playful way.
- 6. **Talk About the Surprise:** Explain that just like how it was tricky to know if the cat was napping or awake while hidden, in a story about a special cat named Schrödinger's cat, it's like the cat is doing two things at once until someone looks at it.
- 7. **Embrace the Surprise:** Encourage the child to appreciate surprises and that sometimes things can be a bit surprising or tricky to guess, just like the playful mystery of Schrödinger's cat!

Chapter 6: Exploring Uncertainty and Duality: A Playful Puzzle Adventure

Hey there, curious minds! Let's dive into a world where surprises reign supreme—where toys play hide-and-seek and guessing games turn into playful mysteries. Welcome to the whimsical playground of uncertainty and duality, where things aren't always what they seem!

Guessing Games Galore

Imagine having a super fun guessing game where things aren't where you'd expect them to be. Picture this: you close your eyes, and your toys vanish into thin air! But wait, they're not gone—just hiding in plain sight. That's a bit like uncertainty, where things aren't predictable, and surprises hide around every corner!

Waves, Particles, and Magical Transformations

Now, let's talk about a playful idea—imagine if your favorite ball could be both bouncy like a ball and flowy like a river at the same time. That's a bit like what happens in the quantum world! Things there can behave like both waves and tiny, zoomy particles, just like your toys sometimes feel like they have magical powers!

Mystery in the Quantum Realm

In the wibbly-wobbly, topsy-turvy world of quantum physics, uncertainty and duality are like playing pretend with your toys. Sometimes, they act super surprising, making you scratch your head in wonder! It's a bit like when you guess where your toy is, and it's not where you thought—but that's the fun part of the game!

Playful Surprises and Puzzling Possibilities

In the magical land of uncertainty and duality, surprises twirl around like your favorite spinning top. Things don't always follow the rules you expect, creating a jigsaw puzzle of giggles and excitement! But that's what makes it an adventure—a chance to explore and giggle at the mysterious and playful side of the quantum world!

Mysteries to Giggle About

So, my playful pals, uncertainty and duality in the quantum world are like secrets waiting to be uncovered. They're puzzles with giggles hidden inside—surprises that make you go, "Wow!" Remember, it's okay not to know everything because in this magical realm, mysteries are like little treasures, waiting for curious explorers like you to discover them!

Activity: Surprise Box

Materials Needed:

- A small box or container with a lid
- Various small toys or objects that fit inside the box (e.g., small plush toys, toy cars, building blocks)

Activity Steps:

- 1. **Prepare the Surprise Box:** Gather the small toys or objects and place them inside the box. Make sure the child doesn't see what's inside. Close the lid securely.
- 2. **Shake and Guess:** Hand the closed box to the child and ask them to guess what might be inside without opening it. Encourage them to use their imagination and guess based on the sounds or feelings when they shake the box.
- 3. **Unveil the Surprise:** After guessing, open the box to reveal the contents. Discuss with the child if their guesses were correct or if they were surprised by what was inside. Talk about how it's sometimes tricky to predict what's inside a closed box just by shaking or guessing.
- 4. **Discussion Time:** Explain in simple terms that sometimes surprises or unpredictability can be fun, just like not knowing what's in the box until it's opened. Relate this idea to the uncertainty principle, mentioning that in the quantum world, there are surprises or things we can't predict about tiny particles.

- 5. **Embrace Surprises:** Encourage the child to appreciate surprises and unexpected things in everyday life, just like the surprise of discovering what's inside the box. Emphasize that it's okay not to know everything and that surprises can be exciting!

Chapter 7: Unraveling the Double-Slit Mystery: A Fun Experiment Adventure

Hey there, curious minds! Imagine a magical game where things change just by peeking—welcome to the exciting world of the double-slit experiment! This experiment is like a playful puzzle that shows us how sneaky particles behave when they think no one's watching. Let's dive into this curious adventure together!

The Mysterious Game Begins

Imagine setting up a special game—let's call it the Double-Slit Game! You invite tiny, zoomy particles to play, but here's the twist: they act super tricky! When no one's looking, they zoom through two tiny holes, like they're saying, "Catch us if you can!" But when you peek, they switch their game plan—oh, what a puzzling play!

The Sneaky Particle Dance

In this wibbly-wobbly experiment, particles act like secret agents, doing a surprise dance when no one's watching! They zoom through the holes and create a cool pattern on the other side, almost like they're painting with tiny paint brushes. But when someone tries to peek, they shy away, changing their dance steps. It's a playful particle dance-off!

Peek-a-Boo, Particles!

Let's play a game of peek-a-boo with these sneaky particles! When you try to catch them in the act, they change their moves, creating a whole new pattern on the wall. It's as if they're saying, "Aha! You can't see us now!" Their playful dance changes whenever someone tries to sneak a peek, leaving behind a trail of giggles and mystery.

Fun with Tiny Surprises

In the super cool world of the double-slit experiment, particles keep surprising us like playful little friends! Their mischievous ways show us that they can act differently when we're not looking. It's like having a secret that only particles know—making this experiment a delightful game full of twists and turns!

Playful Particle Puzzles

So, my playful pals, the double-slit experiment is like a magical game where particles do the silliest dances and create secret patterns. It's a puzzling mystery that teaches us that particles can be a bit shy when they know we're peeking. Remember, even the tiniest particles love a good game of hide-and-seek!

Activity: Wavy Water

Materials Needed:

- A shallow, rectangular container (like a baking pan or a plastic tray)
- Water
- Two thin barriers (these can be pieces of cardboard or paper)
- A flashlight or a small, bright light source (like a phone's flashlight)

Activity Steps:

- 1. **Set Up the Experiment:** Fill the shallow container with water, about halfway. Place it on a stable surface.
- 2. **Create the Barriers:** Take the pieces of cardboard or paper and place them vertically in the water, leaving a small gap between them. Ensure the barriers are close enough so that they create two openings or slits in the water.
- 3. **Let the Light Shine:** Position the flashlight or bright light source to shine light towards the barriers in the water. Adjust the angle so that the light passes through the gaps between the barriers.
- 4. **Observe the Patterns:** Turn off the room lights or darken the area around the container. Look at the patterns created by the light passing through the gaps. You should see alternating bands or patterns of light and shadow on the surface opposite the light source.
- 5. **Experiment with Waves:** Now, gently move the barriers closer together or farther apart. Observe how the patterns on the surface change as you adjust the gaps between the barriers. Notice how the

light behaves differently based on the width of the gaps.
- 6. **Discussion Time:** The experiment with the water and light shows a bit like the double-slit experiment in the quantum world. Just like how the light created patterns when passing through the barriers, particles also create patterns when passing through slits, showing both wave-like and particle-like behavior!
- 7. **Encourage Exploration:** Play with the barriers and observe how changing the width affects the patterns. Notice how the light behaves differently depending on the setup.

Chapter 8: Quantum Superposition: The Wondrous Trick of Being Everywhere!

Hey, curious minds! Imagine if you could be in two places at the same time—sounds like a magical adventure, right? Well, welcome to the incredible world of quantum superposition, where things can do the most amazing disappearing-reappearing acts!

Let's dive into this mind-bending idea together using a playful analogy that'll make it super easy to understand!

The Marvelous Vanishing Act

Imagine you're a magician, and you have a special trick up your sleeve—let's call it the Disappearing-Reappearing Magic! You step into a magical box and say the magic words: "Presto, change-o!" Poof! You vanish! But wait, here's the twist: you also appear on the other side of the room at the same time! That's a bit like what happens in the quantum world!

The Sneaky Quantum Magic

In the amazing world of quantum physics, tiny particles do the most incredible tricks! They can be in two places at once, just like your magical disappearing-reappearing act. Picture this: a particle here and also there, doing a playful dance of "I'm here, I'm there, I'm everywhere!" It's a giggle-inducing magic show of particles!

Juggling Two Places at Once

Now, imagine you're juggling two balls at the same time—one in each hand. That's a bit like what particles do in the quantum world! They can juggle being in two places simultaneously, just like you juggle those balls. It's a super-duper balancing act of particles that'll leave you scratching your head in wonder!

Superposition: The Quantum Showstopper

In the enchanting realm of quantum superposition, particles put on the grandest show! They can be like two friends at two different parties, having fun at both places at the same time. It's like having a twin who can be in two places, doing two different things simultaneously—it's that mind-blowing!

Quantum Magic Unleashed!

So, my fantastic friends, quantum superposition is like having a magic wand that makes things appear in two places at once! It's a playful trick that particles do in the quantum world, leaving us in awe and wonder. Remember, even in the quantum world, the coolest magic shows are full of surprises!

Activity: Magic Juggling Act

Materials Needed:

- Three different-colored balls or toys (e.g., small plush toys, balls, or building blocks)

Activity Steps:

- 1. **Gather the Toys:** Collect three different-colored toys or balls. Make sure they're easy to hold and toss around.
- 2. **Pick a Spot:** Find a comfortable space where you can move around freely without any breakable items nearby.

- 3. **The Juggling Game:** Start by holding two toys in one hand and the third in the other hand.
- 4. **Juggle Like Magic:** Begin tossing the toys gently in the air. But here's the fun part—instead of catching them, pretend they're all in the air at once! Move your hands to mimic catching the toys, but don't actually catch them. Keep them 'suspended' in the air using playful gestures.
- 5. **Counting the Toys:** Ask the child how many toys they see in the air. They might say three, even though you're pretending to hold them all at once.
- 6. **Reveal the Magic:** Explain that just like the toys seemed to be in two places at once during the juggling game, in the quantum world, tiny particles can act in a similar way—being in two places or states simultaneously!
- 7. **Repeat and Explore**: Encourage the child to try the 'magic juggling' act themselves. Let them pretend to suspend all the toys in the air at once and see how many they can visualize.

Chapter 9: Quantum Entanglement: The Incredible Twin Connection of Particles!

Hey there, curious explorers! Let's dive into a mind-boggling world where particles do the most amazing magic trick of all time—quantum entanglement! Imagine having a secret connection, just like how friends share secret messages. Well, in the quantum world, particles do the same—it's like having a special twin connection that's super-duper cool!

The Twin Telepathy Game

Imagine you and a friend have a magical connection, like secret twin telepathy! Your friend goes far, far away, to the moon, maybe, while you stay on Earth. Now, here's the fantastic part: when you think of a special word, your friend instantly knows it! That's a bit like how particles share secrets in the quantum world—they're connected no matter how far apart!

Spooky Actions at a Distance

In the enchanting land of quantum physics, particles have a super mysterious bond called entanglement. It's like having a pair of magical socks—if you pull one, the other one moves, even if they're in different drawers! When something happens to one particle, the other reacts instantly, as if they're sharing a secret handshake across galaxies. It's a bit spooky, but oh-so-fascinating!

The Quantum Teleportation Dance

Now, picture this: particles do a playful dance where one does a spin, and the other twirls at the same time—even if they're galaxies apart! It's like having a synchronized dance party where moves match instantly. That's the magical world of entangled particles—a dance of mysterious connection that's absolutely out of this world!

The Twin Connection's Mystery

In the fantastical world of quantum entanglement, particles act like best buddies who know each other's secrets. Even if they're on opposite ends of the universe, they talk without using words—it's a secret language of particles! Their connection is like having a special phone line that works without wires, instantly passing messages like a lightning bolt.

Quantum Twin Secrets Revealed!

So, my amazing pals, quantum entanglement is like having a secret twin language between particles, making them the best friends of the quantum world. They share secrets instantly, no matter how far apart they are, creating a magical connection that'll leave you grinning in wonder! Remember, even particles have best friend secrets!

Activity: Quantum Twin Dance

Materials Needed:

- Two colorful ribbons or strings of equal length (different colors or patterns work well)
- A partner or a friend

Activity Steps:

- 1. **Get Set:** Choose a partner or a friend to do this activity with you. Each person holds one end of a ribbon or string, making sure they are equal in length.

- 2. **Twirl and Dance:** Stand a few steps away from each other. Now, start moving around while holding onto your ends of the ribbons. As you move, twirl and dance around in different directions, making playful moves with the ribbons.
- 3. **Mirroring Moves:** Try to mirror each other's movements using the ribbons. If one person twirls the ribbon, the other person should try to do the same. It's like doing a dance routine, but with ribbons!
- 4. **Connected Moves:** Here's the fun part! Even when you're both far apart, try moving in a way that the ribbons seem to respond to each other's movements. For example, if one person makes a big loop with their ribbon, the other person should try to do something similar at the same time.
- 5. **Observing the Connection:** After dancing and twirling with the ribbons, take a moment to notice how your moves seem connected. Discuss with your friend how, even though you're holding separate ends of the ribbons, your movements affected each other's actions!
- 6. **The Entangled Ribbons:** Explain that this activity shows a bit like how entangled particles behave. Just like how you and your friend's moves with the ribbons seemed connected, entangled particles act in sync with each other, no matter how far apart they are!

Conclusion: Our Quantum Journey!

Congratulations, fellow adventurers! We've completed an incredible journey into the fascinating world of quantum physics. Together, we've unraveled the mysteries of atoms, peeked inside their tiny worlds, and discovered the magic of molecules and the ever-changing nature of matter. But our journey doesn't end here—it's just the beginning of our quest for knowledge and wonder!

We've embarked on a whirlwind tour through some mind-bending ideas in the quantum realm—Schrödinger's playful cat, the puzzling principles of uncertainty and duality, the curious double-slit experiment, and the fantastic phenomena of superposition and entanglement. These ideas might seem a bit puzzling, but they're the keys to understanding our amazing universe!

Remember, the quantum world is full of surprises and mysteries waiting to be explored. It's okay if some ideas still seem a little tricky—science is all about asking questions and seeking answers!

As we wrap up this adventure, keep your curious spirit alive. Keep asking questions, keep exploring, and never stop wondering about the world around you. Who knows, maybe someday you'll uncover even more incredible secrets hidden in the quantum realm!

So, fellow adventurers, until our next journey into the wonders of science, keep imagining, keep exploring, and keep embracing the magic of discovery. The quantum world awaits your curious minds!

Farewell for now, quantum explorers!

Your feedback is greatly appreciated!

It's through your feedback, support and reviews that I'm able to create the best books possible and serve more people.

I would be extremely grateful if you could take just 60 seconds to kindly leave an honest review of the book on Amazon. Please share your feedback and thoughts for others to see.

To do so, simply find the book on Amazon's website (or wherever you purchased the book from) and locate the section to leave a review. Select a star rating and write a couple of sentences.

That's it! Thank you so much for your support.

Conclusion: Our Quantum Journey!

Review this product

Share your thoughts with other customers

Write a customer review

Bonus Experiments: Uncover the Magic of Quantum Physics!

Experiment 1: Colorful Light Show with a Prism

Step 1: Gather your magical prism and a flashlight!
Get ready to uncover the magic of light that's connected to our quantum journey! Find a prism—a special crystal—and a flashlight.

Step 2: Let the light shine through!
Hold the prism in the sunlight or shine the flashlight through it. This magical crystal splits the light into colors, just like how we discovered in our quantum adventure that light behaves both as waves and particles.

Step 3: Watch the magic unfold!
The light passes through the prism and transforms into a beautiful, colorful rainbow on the wall! Remember how we learned about the duality of light in our quantum journey? This experiment shows how light behaves like both waves and tiny particles called photons.

Experiment 2: Magnetic Exploration Adventure

Step 1: Gather your magnetic treasures!
Get ready to uncover the mysterious forces that connect to quantum physics! Find magnets—those cool things that attract and repel each other.

Step 2: Let's play with attraction and repulsion!
Watch how the magnets stick together or push away. It's a bit like quantum entanglement where particles can be connected, even when far apart! These invisible forces show us a bit about the spooky actions happening between particles in the quantum world.

Experiment 3: Sound Waves Jam Session

Step 1: Join the music band—grab your instruments!
Get ready to explore vibrations, just like particles in the quantum world! Pick instruments or use your magical voice.

Step 2: Let's make some noise!
Play your instruments or sing your favorite song. Feel the vibrations—just like how particles vibrate in the quantum world. Listen closely to the magical world of sound waves, much like how we explored waves in our quantum journey.

Experiment 4: Coin Flipping Fun & Probability Play

Step 1: Get your lucky coins ready!
Let's dive into probability—the chance of something happening.

Find shiny coins—these relate to the uncertainty principle in quantum physics!

Step 2: Flip, flip, hooray!
Flip the coin and see if it lands heads or tails. Discuss the chances, much like how quantum physics deals with probabilities and uncertain outcomes in the quantum realm.

Experiment 5: Shadow Play & Light Magic Show

Step 1: Gather your magical light source!
Time for shadow fun that connects to our quantum exploration! Find a light source like a lamp or flashlight.

Step 2: Time for shadow magic!
Shine the light on objects and watch shadows appear. Explore how light interacts with objects—just like how we learned about light interacting with particles in our quantum journey, creating mysterious effects like the double-slit experiment.

References

OpenAI. (2023). Conversations with ChatGPT. Retrieved [Jan 9, 2024], from https://www.openai.com/chatgpt/

www.ingramcontent.com/pod-product-compliance
Lightning Source LLC
Chambersburg PA
CBHW071324080526
44587CB00018B/3342